SUPER BOWLS

Hal Rogers

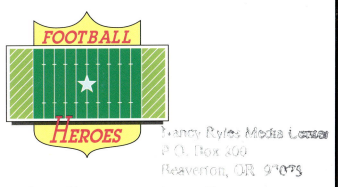

The Rourke Corporation, Inc.
Vero Beach, Florida 32964

The Rourke Corporation, Inc.
P.O. Box 3328, Vero Beach, FL 32964

Rogers, Hal, 1966-
    Super Bowls/by Hal Rogers.
       p. cm. — (Football heroes)
    Includes bibliographical references (p. 47) and index.
    Summary: Discusses the Super Bowl and notable moments in its history.
    ISBN 0-86593-153-4
    1. Super Bowl Game (Football)—History—Juvenile literature. [1. Super Bowl Game (Football)—History.] I. Title II. Series.
GV956.2.S8R64 1992
796.332'648—dc20

                                                            92-8762
                                                              CIP
                                                               AC

Series Editor: Gregory Lee
Editor: Marguerite Aronowitz
Book design and production: The Creative Spark, San Clemente, CA
Cover photograph: Mike Powell/ALLSPORT

Contents

Jeff Hostetler's clutch performance in the 1990 playoffs and Super Bowl XXV helped defeat the Buffalo Bills, 20-19.

Going For Greatness

What makes a football game great? What is it that makes one game more exciting than another? The Super Bowl is a battle between what should be the two best teams of the National Football Conference (NFC) and the American Football Conference (AFC). Ideally, it should be the best game of the year. In 1991, it may well have been.

Super Bowl XXV was a match-up between the Buffalo Bills and the New York Giants, who were without their star quarterback, Phil Simms. Both teams had excellent seasons, although the Bills were seven-point favorites. The suspense lasted right down to the final seconds. This thrilling game saw four lead changes and not a single turnover.

Super Trivia

Q: *Who is the winningest coach in Super Bowl history?*

A: *Chuck Noll, who has coached the Pittsburgh Steelers since 1969, has won all four Super Bowls his team attended. Don Shula, coach of the Miami Dolphins, has coached in more Super Bowls overall. He has been to the big game six times, once as head coach of the Baltimore Colts in 1969 (they lost to the New York Jets), and five times with the Dolphins from 1972 through 1985. He has only won two of his six Super Bowls.*

In 1990 running back Ottis Anderson was the MVP in the New York Giants' second Super Bowl victory. Super Bowl XXV is regarded by many sports fans as the best yet.

Buffalo led 12-3 in the second quarter until Giants' quarterback Jeff Hostetler completed a 14-yard strike to wide receiver Stephen Baker, closing the half 12-10.

In the first play of the fourth quarter, Buffalo's Thurman Thomas ran 31 yards for a touchdown to give Buffalo a 19-17 lead. But the real story of the second half was the way the Giants controlled the ball. They used up lots of time on the game clock, keeping the Bills' offense off the field for precious minutes. Buffalo never had the chance to show what they could do, because the Giants made no mistakes. After a lengthy drive, Giants' kicker Matt Bahr kicked a 21-yard field goal that gave the Giants a 20-19 lead. Both teams played a tight fourth quarter. Then, with just seconds left in the game, Buffalo's kicker Scott Norwood had a chance to win the NFL championship for his team. It was a 47-yard field goal attempt, a hard kick in any situation. But Norwood was an excellent kicker. Time seemed to stand still. Players on the sidelines knelt in tense silence, knowing the game could go to either team. Norwood's kick sailed off to the right, and the officials signaled "no good." The Giants would take home the Vince Lombardi trophy.

Never before had the win or loss of a Super Bowl rested on one player. In Super Bowl V, Jim O'Brien's winning field goal gave the Baltimore Colts the game. But the score was tied when he went to kick. Even if he had missed, the game would not have been over. Joe Montana's thrilling pass against the Bengals in Super Bowl XXIII won the game in the final quarter with 14:26 left to play—not seconds. And that pass came on 2nd-and-2 from the 10-yard line, almost a sure thing for Montana. But in Super Bowl XXV, the hopes of both teams rested on the success or failure of one man with one chance.

Super Bowl XXV lived up to what everyone thought a championship game should be—a hard-fought battle between two great teams with action into the final seconds. Maybe all Super Bowls aren't this thrilling, but the game is still an American tradition.

*The winning Super Bowl team receives the Vince Lombardi Trophy,
named for the coach who won the first two Super Bowls.*

The Tradition Begins

Football is so much a part of American life it's hard to believe that what we know today as the National Football League (NFL) has yet to celebrate its 30th birthday. For five months of every year, fans are glued to their television sets, cheering their favorite teams on to victory or sharing the sorrow of defeat. And while every game of the season is part of the excitement, fans wait all year for the biggest event: the NFL's championship game, the Super Bowl.

From its very first game, the Super Bowl captured the imagination of football fans. Each year nearly 500 million people around the world watch America's biggest one-day sporting event. Five of the top ten highest-rated television shows of all time have been Super Bowls. Ski slopes in Colorado are almost empty on Super Bowl Sunday. California's usually jam-packed freeways run smoothly. Police around the country claim that fewer crimes are committed during the Super Bowl, and hospitals admit less people into emergency rooms. For a few hours every January, the country seems to hold still while two teams battle it out for the NFL championship.

How does a team make it to the Super Bowl? The NFL today is made up of 28 teams. These teams are divided in half into the American Football Conference (AFC) and the National Football Conference (NFC). Each conference is divided into three divisions—Eastern, Central, and Western. Each team plays a schedule of 16 games during the regular season, playing every other team in their division twice. The champions of each division, along with a team from each conference with the next best record (called a *wild card*), meet in the playoffs. Eventually, the winning team from each conference advances to the Super Bowl.

The NFL has been around since 1922, but it used to resemble what we call the NFC today. Only three of the earlier NFL teams still survive, and only the Chicago Bears and Green Bay Packers remain in their original cities. The league was the only major professional football league until 1959, when it was challenged by the up-and-coming American Football League (AFL). The AFL was recruiting the best college players of the day with offers of high wages.

The AFL became popular with football fans because of its young, daring players. The two leagues warred for years, fighting for the fans and the best players. Finally, in 1966, the NFL and AFL agreed to become one professional league ruled by one commissioner. This merger did not become final until 1970, but part of the agreement was that the first championship game between the two leagues would be at the end of the 1966 season.

January 15, 1967 was an historic day—the first Super Bowl. The AFL and the NFL had never met before, even in a scrimmage. It was the AFL's Kansas City Chiefs against the NFL's Green Bay Packers in the first championship game. The rivalry between the two leagues was at its peak. But even with the AFL's powerful passing game and wide-open playing style, the NFL was still considered the better league. And Green Bay had just won three straight NFL championships before the merger. No one expected much of a game. In fact, the first championship game had the smallest crowd in the history of the Super Bowl—only 61,946 people.

Coach Vince Lombardi of the Green Bay Packers, one of the most respected football coaches of all time, was in a tough position. Everyone expected his team to win, so a loss to the AFL would have been embarrassing. The first half was close. The Chiefs scored a touchdown and a field goal, and the half ended with the Packers ahead only 14-10. But with the passing of quarterback great Bart Starr, the receiving of Max McGee, and a key interception by all-pro safety Willie Wood, Green Bay took control of the game. McGee, a veteran who wasn't expected to play in the game, caught seven passes for 138 yards and two touchdowns. Starr completed 16 of 23 passes for 250 yards and was chosen MVP. Lombardi's Packers beat the upstart Chiefs 35-10.

In case Lombardi's skills as a coach still needed to be proven, he had another chance the following year. The second Super Bowl was a match-up between the Packers and the AFL's Oakland Raiders (now the Los Angeles Raiders). The championship game was gaining popularity quickly. Almost 15,000 more fans went to the second Super Bowl than the first.

The NFL was still the favorite. Although the Oakland Raiders had had a great season, they were no match for "the Pack." It was to be Vince Lombardi's last game as coach of the Green Bay Packers. In tribute to a great coach, his team beat the Raiders 33-14. Lombardi's nine years as the Packers' head coach ended with six Western Conference championships, five NFL championships, and two Super Bowl wins. From that time on, the trophy for the winning Super Bowl team became known as the Vince Lombardi trophy.

The first two Super Bowls set a pattern for many that followed. That is, one team often beats the other by a large score, and it is rarely the most exciting game of the season. Many people complain that the Super Bowl doesn't live up to our high hopes for a thrilling clash

Running back Paul Hornung (above) and quarterback Bart Starr (right) were two stars of the Green Bay Packers' first Super Bowl victory.

between two great teams. But once in a while the Super Bowl is, indeed, the best game of the year. This was the case in 1969.

The AFL's New York Jets faced the NFL's powerful Baltimore Colts, the heavy favorite to win. But the Jets had one of the most exciting young players in the history of football calling their plays: quarterback Joe Namath. His superstar hands made Super Bowl III one of the most exciting sports events ever. From that time on, the Super Bowl became the game fans looked forward to all year.

Joe Namath talked big before Super Bowl III when his team was the underdog—and he backed it up with an MVP performance.

The AFL continued to be the underdog. Bill Curry, who played center for the Colts from 1967 through 1972, remembers how his team felt going into the game. "We were 15 and 1...the only game we'd lost was to the Cleveland Browns. We'd just played Cleveland in Cleveland, had beaten them 34-0 for the NFL title. And now we were going to finish up as the greatest team in history." How did the Colts feel about the AFL? Says Curry, "If you couldn't make it in the NFL, you played for the AFL."

So the Colts felt like they had a sure thing. But then Joe Namath had the nerve to announce to the public that the Jets would win. "We're going to beat the Colts on Sunday," announced Namath. "I *guarantee* it." Because the Colts' star quarterback, Johnny Unitas, had torn his elbow before the regular season, second-stringer Earl Morrall had led the team to their great 15-1 record. But that didn't stop Namath from blasting him to the press. He said there were at least five quarterbacks in the AFL who were better than Morrall.

By game day, the Colts had become 19 ½ point favorites. Namath's teammates were angry about his gutsy promises, but the fans were interested. Tension was high as the two teams came out on the field. In the first half, Morrall threw three interceptions. Namath was cool and confident. While the Colts tried to fight back, the Jets played conservative ball. Namath's longest pass was just 39 yards. He completed 17 of 28 passes and led his team in a steady attack. The Jets scored a touchdown in both the second and third quarters, while the Colts couldn't make it onto the scoreboard. Finally, in the fourth quarter, Johnny Unitas replaced Morrall. He gave the Colts their only touchdown. But it was too late. The Jets scored a field goal and won the game 16-7. Things had changed— an AFL team was king of football. And the Super Bowl was now a tradition.

With the explosive running of Larry Csonka, the Miami Dolphins became the second team to win back-to-back Super Bowls.

Into The Seventies

The national championship game still didn't have a name. We look back at the first three games between the AFL and the NFL and call them Super Bowls, but that colorful title was not used until 1971. Why is it called the Super Bowl? The answer is surprising. One evening, an AFL official named Lamar Hunt came home to find his daughter playing with a small ball that bounced like crazy. He asked her what it was. She called it a "super ball." Hunt began calling the championship game the Super Bowl, and little by little so did everyone else.

After the David and Goliath battle of Super Bowl III, fans had high hopes for the 1970 championship. This was the last real battle between the two separate leagues, because in the following year the merger would be complete. The AFL Kansas City Chiefs were back, this time facing the Minnesota Vikings, a team that won four NFL conference titles in the 1970s. Unfortunately, the fans weren't treated to the thrills of the year before. In an uneventful game, the Chiefs beat Minnesota 23-7. But the AFL had now won back-to-back championships.

In 1971, the NFL became the league we know today, made up of the AFC and the NFC. The NFC Colts were still licking their wounds from their Super Bowl III loss when they met the Dallas Cowboys in Super Bowl V. The game was close, but not terribly exciting. But as the fourth quarter came to an end, the fans got an edge-of-the seat finish. During the regular season it isn't unusual for a game to be decided in the final seconds by a field goal. Super Bowl V was the first one to end with just such a field goal—and it wouldn't happen again for 20 years. In the final five seconds of the game, Colts' first-year kicker Jim O'Brien kicked a 32-yard field goal six feet inside the upright. The Colts were victorious, 16-13.

The Dallas Cowboys didn't take this defeat lightly. Led by head coach Tom Landry and superstar quarterback Roger Staubach, when they returned to the Super Bowl the next year, they were the team to beat. But in fact, the Miami Dolphins didn't put up much of a fight, as the Cowboys rushed for a record 252 yards and their crushing defense made the Dolphins the only team in Super Bowl history to leave the game without scoring a touchdown.

The Miami Dolphins might not have done well in their first Super Bowl, but in 1973 they had a perfect season—they won every game they played. For the next two years they owned the NFL title, becoming the first team to attend three consecutive Super Bowls.

In Super Bowl VII, the Dolphins beat the Washington Redskins to win their first NFL

Dallas Cowboys' head coach Tom Landry and quarterback Roger Staubach won Super Bowls VI and XII together.

championship title. Miami played an almost perfect half, with their defense permitting the Skins to cross midfield only once. Miami's Larry Csonka, one of the best running backs of all time, ran 112 yards on just 15 carries. The Dolphin offense turned good field goal position into two touchdowns to end the half with a 14-0 lead. Neither team scored in the second half until, with only seven minutes left in the game, one of football's most famous blunders took place.

The Dolphins lined up for a 42-yard field goal attempt. The snap was low, and Washington's Bill Brundige blocked the kick. Miami kicker Garo Yepremian (whose field goal scored Miami's only points in Super Bowl VI) picked up the loose ball and attempted to pass it. Instead, the ball slipped from his hands and the Redskins' Mike Bass ran the ball 49 yards for a touchdown, the longest return of a recovered fumble in Super Bowl history. The Dolphins still won the game, but Yepremian's mistake prevented what might have been the only shutout in a Super Bowl.

A third stellar year brought the Dolphins back to the Super Bowl in 1974. This time they met the Minnesota Vikings. Miami scored on their first possession. Larry Csonka, the star of the field again, bolted in for a five-yard touchdown after a 10-play drive. Just four plays later, the Dolphins had the ball back and scored on another 10-play drive. Later, Garo Yepremian supplied a 28-yard field goal.

While the Dolphin's offense was doing their part, the defense was working just as hard, holding the Vikings to only seven plays in the first quarter. Near the end of the half, the Vikings were on the Miami seven-yard line with 1:18 left on the board—their first real scoring chance. Then Dolphin linebacker Nick Buoniconti jarred the ball loose, Miami recovered, and the Minnesota threat was over. The game ended with a score of 24-7. Csonka rushed an amazing 33 times for 145 yards—then a Super Bowl record—winning the MVP award. "He is," Minnesota quarterback Fran Tarkenton admitted, "the greatest fullback I have ever seen." Together with a killer defensive squad, Csonka led the Dolphins to two straight Super Bowl wins.

By 1974, there was a new power emerging in the AFC—the Pittsburgh Steelers. They had a deadly defense known as the Steel Curtain. Led by a great tackle called "Mean" Joe Greene, the Steeler defense terrified opponents for most of the '70s. In Super Bowl IX, the Curtain handed the Vikings their third Super Bowl loss. The Steelers' intimidating defense crippled the Vikings, leaving them with an all-time Super Bowl low of just 17 yards rushing! The Steelers gained 333 yards, including Franco Harris' 158 yards on 34 carries (a new record). But the final score was just 16-6.

The following year was a classic confrontation. The Steelers were back for Super Bowl X, this time to battle it out against the popular Cowboys. This was a meeting not just of two great teams, but of two of the game's top quarterbacks: the Cowboys' Roger Staubach and the Steelers' Terry Bradshaw. Both superstars hurled two touchdowns. But it was Bradshaw who stole the show by completing a spectacular 64-yard touchdown pass to the invincible receiver Lynn Swann. Unfortunately, Bradshaw never saw Swann's incredible catch. Dallas safety Cliff Harris knocked Bradshaw unconscious just as he let the ball go!

Swann's catch is one of the most exciting moments ever witnessed in the Super Bowl. But before Super Bowl X, it didn't look like Swann would play in the big game because of a concussion he'd suffered earlier. In fact, Cliff Harris tried to scare Swann the week before the game when he was interviewed by the press. "I said to myself, 'How dare he?'" Swann remembers. "If he hadn't said those things, I might have stayed out." Unfortunately for the Cowboys, Swann did play, made four impressive catches, and set a Super Bowl record by gaining 161 yards on four receptions and winning the MVP honor. Surprisingly, Swann hadn't caught a single pass in Super Bowl IX the year before!

The Steelers followed Swann's spectacular catch with 36- and 18-yard field goals by kicker Roy Gerela, and a safety by Reggie Harrison. They were ahead 21-17, but Dallas didn't give up. In a late rally, the Cowboys made their way up the field until—in the final play of the game—Roger Staubach's pass was intercepted in the end zone. The Steelers had a tight hold on the Vince Lombardi trophy for the second year in a row.

In 1977, a record 81 million television viewers watched the Oakland Raiders meet the Minnesota Vikings in Super Bowl XI. The undaunted Vikings were NFC champions for the fourth time, but still without a Super Bowl win. And this year they were about to face a nasty defense and a record-breaking offense. The Raiders won the game 32-14, leaving the Vikings with a fourth Super Bowl loss, a record now tied only by the Denver Broncos. In Fran Tarkenton's 18-year career (1961-78), he completed more passes for more yards and more touchdowns than any other quarterback in NFL history. As many a sports writer notes, Tarkenton—known as "Scramblin' Fran"—is the greatest player in Super Bowl history who never won the big one.

By the late '70s it seemed that the national title was in the hands of the AFC, particularly the Dolphins and Steelers. And the Raiders had come on strong in Super Bowl XI. In 1978, however, a new team showed up. The Denver Broncos made it to their first Super Bowl by beating the Steelers in a tough playoff game. They were up against "America's team," the Dallas Cowboys.

The grace of Lynn Swann made him a Super Bowl MVP during the Pittsburgh Steelers era.

Hall of Fame quarterback Terry Bradshaw and the awesome Pittsburgh Steelers were a dynasty in the 1970s, winning four Super Bowls.

The game was played in the Louisiana Superdome—the first indoor Super Bowl. The Dallas defense put together a frightening four-man rush against Denver quarterback Craig Morton. In the first quarter alone he threw four interceptions and handed the Cowboys a 13-0 lead. Morton completed only four of 15 passes, and when he started the second quarter with another near interception, he was replaced by quarterback Norris Weese. Weese led the Broncos to their only touchdown in a 27-10 defeat.

The NFC was back on top after Super Bowl XII. Dallas hoped to keep the NFL championship title when they returned to the Bowl in 1979 against the Steelers in the first-ever Super Bowl rematch. America watched as two powerhouses went to war.

In the first quarter Bradshaw threw two Steeler touchdown passes to John Stallworth, and a third to Rocky Blier with 26 seconds remaining in the half. Staubach, too, performed well in the first half, completing two Dallas touchdown passes. The teams entered the second half with the Steelers ahead 21-14. The game stayed tight through the third quarter, but in the fourth quarter the Steelers scored two touchdowns in a span of 19 seconds. Steeler Franco Harris made a 22-yard run to put the Steelers ahead 28-17 with 7:10 left to play. After a Dallas fumble, Bradshaw connected with Lynn Swann on an 18-yard pass to bring the lead to 35-17.

A team with less drive than the Cowboys might have given up. With just 2:23 left in the game, Staubach fired a touchdown pass to Billy Joe DuPree. Then the Cowboys recovered an onside kick. Staubach's passing skill resulted in another score with 22 seconds remaining. It was now 35-31, but time ran out. Rocky Blier recovered another onside kick and the game was over. The Steelers won.

What a game! Bradshaw had hurled a record four touchdown passes and completed 17 of 30 for 318 yards—a personal high. The Cowboys had rallied for an electrifying fourth quarter. The Steelers were the first team to win three Super Bowls. The last Super Bowl of the '70s left the public waiting impatiently for football to move into the next decade.

*Joe Montana, leader of the San Francisco 49ers, won four
Super Bowls in the 1980s.*

The Eighties: From East To West

The AFC seemed to own the Super Bowl in the 1970s, much to the embarrassment of the more experienced NFC. The Dolphins and the Steelers—both teams from the eastern United States—had formed dynasties that devastated NFC opponents nearly every time they met in the NFL championship. And when the Pittsburgh Steelers marched into Super Bowl XIV—the first Super Bowl of the '80s—it looked as though things were not about to change.

This time the Steelers were pitted against the Los Angeles Rams. It was to be the last time the Steelers dynasty would make it to the Super Bowl. The players were getting older, and fresh young teams were waiting in the wings, anxious to topple the old regime. The game was close, but in the third quarter the Rams' Nolan Cromwell dropped an interception that might have won the game. Then, surprisingly, Bradshaw threw two back-to-back interceptions. But true to form, he cleaned up his act and the Steelers went on to win 31-19.

In this game, Bradshaw had completed 14 of 21 passes for 309 yards and set career Super Bowl records for the most touchdown passes (nine) and the most passing yards (932). Franco Harris became the number one rusher in Super Bowl history. The Pittsburgh

Steelers became the first team to win four Super Bowls.

In 1981, Super Bowl XV marked the first time a "wild card" team won the game. The Oakland Raiders met the Philadelphia Eagles, who were NFC champs for the first time. Jim Plunkett had become the Raiders' starting quarterback in the sixth game of the season, winning nine of 11 games. Oakland didn't win the division championship, but they qualified as a wild card. Plunkett played an outstanding Super Bowl, including an 80-yard pass—then the longest touchdown pass in the game's history. Oakland linebacker Rod Martin intercepted three passes for a Super Bowl record, crippling the Eagle offense. The Raiders had stuck it out to win their second Super Bowl 27-10.

In 1982, the San Francisco 49ers—a West Coast team—reached the Super Bowl for the first time in club history. Super Bowl XVI matched them against the Cincinnati Bengals, another first-time league champion. The first half was pitifully one-sided. The 49ers struck first with quarterback Joe Montana's one-yard touchdown run ending a 68-yard drive. Next, Earl Cooper caught an 11-yard scoring pass, capping a record 92-yard drive on 12 plays. Finally, Ray Wersching kicked two field goals to give San Francisco a 20-0 lead over the stunned Bengals at the end of the half.

Cincinnati coach Forrest Gregg must have set a fire under his players in the locker room at half time. The Bengals bounced back in the second half as quarterback Ken Anderson ran in one touchdown and connected with Dan Ross for another, bringing the score to 20-14. But Wersching added early fourth-quarter field goals to bring the 49ers' lead to 26-14. Then, with 16 seconds remaining, Anderson completed another pass to Dan Ross for a touchdown, but it wasn't enough. The Bengals lost by a nose, 26-21.

It was a game of records and memories for both

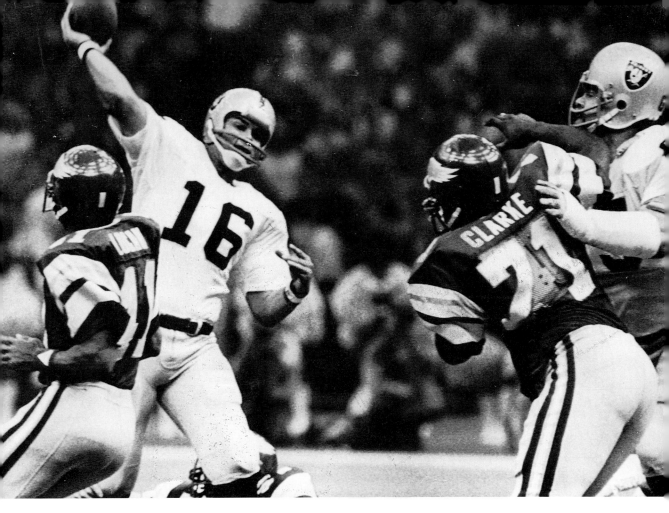

The Oakland Raiders, led by quarterback Jim Plunkett, were the first and only wild card team to win a Super Bowl.

teams. Montana may have been the star of the first half, but it was Anderson who set Super Bowl records for completions (25) and completion percentage (73.5 percent). Montana, the MVP, completed 14 of 22 passes for 157 yards. Bengal receiver Ross set a Super Bowl record with 11 receptions for 104 yards. Cincinnati chalked up 345 yards to San Francisco's 275, marking the first time in Super Bowl history that the team who gained the most yards from scrimmage lost the game.

Super Bowl XVII was a meeting of the NFC's Washington Redskins and the Miami Dolphins in their fourth appearance. Miami built a half-time lead that began with a 76-yard touchdown pass from quarterback David Woodley. Together with a 20-yard field goal and a record 98-yard kickoff return by Fulton Walker that broke a 10-10 tie, the Dolphins were ahead by seven points at the half.

Fullback John Riggins gave Washington its first break with 10:01 left in the game, running 43 yards for a touchdown in a fourth-and-one situation. The Dolphins seemed to shut down as Joe Thiesmann threw a six-yard touchdown pass to Charlie Brown. Riggins made a Super Bowl record 166 yards on 38 carries and helped move the Redskins to a 27-17 victory. NFL/NFC teams had not won two Super Bowls in a row since the back-to-back wins of the Green Bay Packers in the '60s. But the 1980s would belong to the NFC.

Thiesmann, Riggins, and the Redskins were back again in 1984, but their momentum was gone. The Los Angeles Raiders dominated the game from the start, winning 38-9. At the time, it was the most lopsided score in the history of the Super Bowl. Looking back, the '80s would be the decade of the lopsided Super Bowl.

Joe Montana and the San Francisco 49ers returned in Super Bowl XIX to face another great quarterback, Dan Marino of the Miami Dolphins. The first quarter ended with the Dolphins ahead 10-7, the most points scored in the first quarter of any Super Bowl to date. But Montana was warmed up and ready to go in the second quarter, building a 28-16 half-time lead.

49er running back Roger Craig set a Super Bowl record by scoring three touchdowns on pass receptions. By the end of the game Montana had completed 24 of 35 passes for a record 331 yards and three touchdowns. He rushed five times for 59 yards, including a six-yard touchdown. And he won the MVP award for the second time, joining Green Bay's Bart Starr and Pittsburgh's Terry Bradshaw as the only two-time winners of the Most Valuable Player honor. San Francisco also beat out Oakland's record 429 yards from Super Bowl XI to net

Quarterback Dan Marino of the Miami Dolphins was a rising star when he faced the 49ers in his first Super Bowl. The powerful San Francisco team shot the Dolphins down, 38-16.

537 yards. The 49ers were about to become a legend.

Super Bowl XX in 1986 followed the lopsided tradition of the Raiders-Redskin game two years before, when the startling Chicago Bears made their first and only Super Bowl appearance to date. The Bears destroyed the New England Patriots 46-10. It was the biggest blowout in Super Bowl history. But the blowout record would have some serious competition from the Denver Broncos, who became the AFC champs for the next two years.

In Super Bowl XXI, the Broncos faced the New York Giants, a powerful team that had beaten their three playoff opponents by a total of 82 points (Giants 105, opponents 23). Denver was led by the popular quarterback John Elway. The first half was the closest in Super Bowl history, ending with the Broncos ahead 10-9. But the second half belonged to the Giants. They limited Denver to only two yards on 10 offensive plays in the third quarter. Giants' quarterback Phil Simms set Super Bowl records for most consecutive completions (10) and the highest completion percentage (88 percent). He passed for 268 yards and three touchdowns, and the Giants won 39-20.

The following year the Broncos were back with a vengeance, promising to beat the Washington Redskins. Unfortunately, Super Bowl XXII was even harder on Denver than the year before. Elway's team started strong with a 56-yard touchdown, followed by a field goal. But those 10 points would be their last of the game. Washington had a record-setting second quarter, gaining 35 points on five straight possessions. The game was all but over when Washington scored one more touchdown to bring the final score to 42-10—another blowout of the '80s.

It was a record-setting game. Redskins' quarterback Doug Williams had surpassed Joe Montana's

Chicago running back Walter Payton has the most rushing yardage in NFL history (16,726 yards), but he only got to play in the Super Bowl once: during his last pro season, 1986.

Bears' quarterback Jim McMahon celebrates as William "The Refrigerator" Perry shuts down the Patriot's goal-line stand.

The most frustrated head coach in the NFL must be Dan Reeves, who has led his Denver Broncos to three Super Bowl appearances—and lost them all.

previous Super Bowl record with 340 yards passing. Wide receiver Ricky Sanders ended with 193 yards on eight catches, beating Lynn Swann's achievement. Rookie running back Timmy Smith broke Marcus Allen's record with 204 yards rushing. And Washington's six touchdowns and 602 total yards were also new Super Bowl all-time highs.

The Broncos didn't return to 1989's Super Bowl XXIII, much to the relief of football fans around the country. But Joe Montana and the 49ers did—for their third NFL championship. It was a rematch with the Cincinnati Bengals, their opponent in the hard-fought Super Bowl XVI. At half time the score was 3-3, the

Jerry Rice's pass receptions helped put the 49ers into the Super Bowl.

first-ever tie at the half in a Super Bowl. Both teams kicked field goals in the third quarter, but then the Bengals moved ahead with a 93-yard kickoff return for a touchdown. The 49ers answered back with an 85-yard drive in four plays, ending with a 14-yard pass to wide receiver Jerry Rice.

The score was tied 13-13 when Cincinnati's Jim Breech kicked a 40-yard field goal with 3:20 remaining. Starting at the eight-yard line, San Francisco rallied for one of the greatest drives in Super Bowl history. For 92 yards, Montana was working at the peak of his game. With 34 seconds remaining he threw a 10-yard pass to wide receiver John Taylor. San Francisco won 20-16 in a hair-raising finish. Rice was named MVP with 11 catches for a record 215 yards. Montana set yet another record with 357 yards, beating Doug Williams' record from the previous year. The San Francisco 49ers took home the Vince Lombardi trophy for the third time in the last Super Bowl of the '80s, becoming the first NFC team to win three Super Bowls. There was no question that Montana and the 49ers were the stars of the decade.

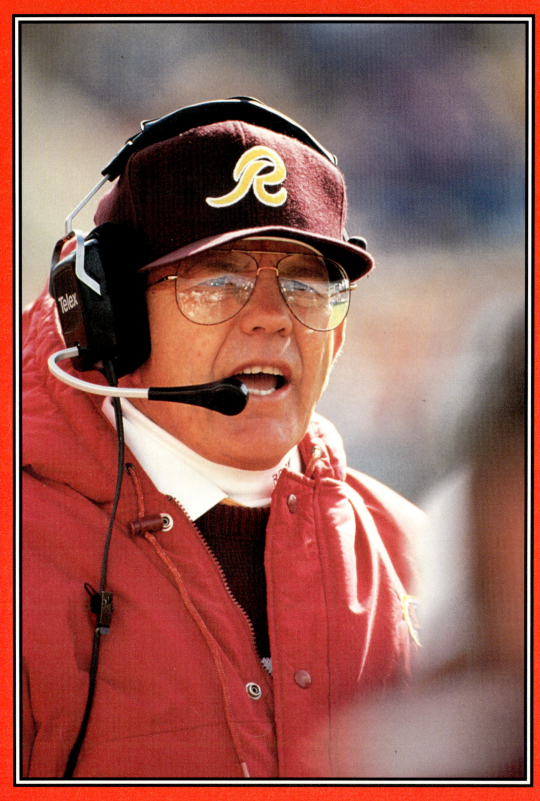

Behind every Super Bowl team is a great coach. The Redskins' Joe Gibbs won his third Super Bowl in 1992 against the Bills.

The Nineties
And Beyond

The lopsided match-ups in several Super Bowls in the 1980s made fans wonder about the quality of the teams who made it to the championship. But there had also been some hard-fought battles between skilled teams that kept the fans glued to their televisions. By 1990 the Super Bowl had become an international event. What will the '90s hold in store?

The first three games of the 1990s were as different as night and day. One was a blowout featuring the jinxed Denver Broncos, and another was arguably one of the best Super Bowls ever.

In 1990 San Francisco was back again in Super Bowl XXIV facing Denver. While the 49ers were Super Bowl champions of the '80s, the Broncos had become the no-win Vikings of the same decade. The match-up sparked a lot of jokes,

Super Trivia

Q: *Name the players who have scored the most career Super Bowl points.*

A: *There are three players—Franco Harris of the Steelers, and Roger Craig and Jerry Rice, both of the 49ers. All scored 24 points in the NFL championship.*

Q: *What quarterback has completed the most Super Bowl passes throughout his career?*

A: *Joe Montana, the 49ers general, has completed 83 of 122 passes during his Super Bowl Sundays. Eleven of these passes turned into touchdowns.*

Broncos star John Elway has yet to wear a Super Bowl ring.

and everyone expected a one-sided game.

They guessed right. San Francisco scored on four of its six first-half possessions to hold a 27-3 lead at the half. Quarterback John Elway was intercepted in the Broncos' first two possessions of the second half. San Francisco won its fourth Super Bowl championship with a 55-10 victory, tying the Pittsburgh Steelers for most Super Bowl wins. Their 55 points broke the previous winning margin in a Super Bowl of 46 points by Chicago in Super Bowl XX. Montana threw a record five touchdowns. He was once again named MVP, winning the award more times than any other player in Super Bowl history. The game was a superb exhibition—by one team.

The next year, Super Bowl XXV won back the devotion of disappointed football fans who were losing faith in the big game. The non-stop action between the Buffalo Bills and the New York Giants is now considered classic football. The Bill's heart-breaking loss may have seemed a little less painful the following year when their superior playing brought them back to Super Bowl XXVI. Unfortunately, the trophy was still out of reach.

The Bills were plagued by error after error. They fumbled on the opening kickoff. Buffalo tailback Thurman Thomas, the NFL's most valuable player, had to sit out for the first two plays because he couldn't find his helmet. And the day didn't improve—Thomas rushed only 10 times for 13 yards, 121 less than in last year's Super Bowl. Quarterback Jim Kelly was sacked five times and intercepted four times. Recievers dropped passes. Penalties were called at crucial moments.

The Redskins' Mark Rypien passed for 292 yards and two touchdowns and completed 18 of 33 attempts to lead his team to their 37-24 victory. After a slow first quarter, the Redskins came back in the second with the drive to win. In less than six minutes, they achieved a

Mark Rypien celebrates after a Redskins' touchdown during their 37-24 defeat of the Bills in Super Bowl XXVI.

17-0 lead. First there was a 34-yard field goal. Then Rypien hit Earnest Byner for a 10-yard touchdown play. Then Darrell Green picked off Jim Kelly, and Gerald Riggs scored from one yard out. After the Bills received a penalty, the Skins went on to make another touchdown to bring the score to 24-0.

From there, the Bills made a touchdown and a field goal to hit the scoreboard. But the Redskins weren't ready to stop. After a great drive, Rypien threw a perfect pass to Gary Clark for a 30-yard touchdown, giving Washington a 31-10 lead before the end of the third quarter. The 1991 victory marked the Redskins third Super Bowl victory in 10 years. Coach Joe Gibbs has seen three championships in four tries with three different quarterbacks—Rypien, Joe Thiesmann, and Doug Williams.

Sometimes the Super Bowl is, indeed, super. Other times, it isn't the best way to finish a long season. There's no way of knowing until the game starts just how exciting a match of two teams will be. Who's to say what will happen to the big game as we move further into the '90s? Will the NFC continue to dominate? Will the AFC come back and be the force it was in the '70s? Will we continue to have uneven matches and lopsided scores, with the occasional head-to-head combat between two greats? We'll have to wait and see.

One thing is for sure. We'll all be there for the coin toss year in and year out. Whether we're glued to the television set or lucky enough to be there in person, there's no question—football fans are crazy about the Super Bowl.

Super Bowl Results, 1967-1992

Bowl	Date	Winner	Loser	Score
I	1-15-67	Green Bay Packers	Kansas City Chiefs	35-10
II	1-14-68	Green Bay Packers	Oakland Raiders	33-14
III	1-12-69	New York Jets	Baltimore Colts	16-7
IV	1-11-70	Kansas City Chiefs	Minnesota Vikings	23-7
V	1-17-71	Baltimore Colts	Dallas Cowboys	16-13
VI	1-16-72	Dallas Cowboys	Miami Dolphins	24-3
VII	1-14-73	Miami Dolphins	Washington Redskins	14-7
VIII	1-13-74	Miami Dolphins	Minnesota Vikings	24-7
IX	1-12-75	Pittsburgh Steelers	Minnesota Vikings	16-6
X	1-18-76	Pittsburgh Steelers	Dallas Cowboys	21-17
XI	1-9-77	Oakland Raiders	Minnesota Vikings	32-14
XII	1-15-78	Dallas Cowboys	Denver Broncos	27-10
XIII	1-21-79	Pittsburgh Steelers	Dallas Cowboys	35-31
XIV	1-20-80	Pittsburgh Steelers	Los Angeles Rams	31-19
XV	1-25-81	Oakland Raiders	Philadelphia Eagles	27-10
XVI	1-24-82	San Francisco 49ers	Cincinnati Bengals	26-21
XVII	1-30-83	Washington Redskins	Miami Dolphins	27-17
XVIII	1-22-84	Los Angeles Raiders	Washington Redskins	38-9
XIX	1-20-85	San Francisco 49ers	Miami Dophins	38-16
XX	1-26-86	Chicago Bears	New England Patriots	46-10
XXI	1-25-87	New York Giants	Denver Broncos	39-20
XXII	1-31-88	Washington Redskins	Denver Broncos	42-10
XXIII	1-22-89	San Fancisco 49ers	Cincinnati Bengals	20-16
XXIV	1-28-90	San Francisco 49ers	Denver Broncos	55-10
XXV	1-27-91	New York Giants	Buffalo Bills	20-19
XXVI	1-26-92	Washington Redskins	Buffalo Bills	37-24

Stats

All-Time Super Bowl Leaders: Touchdown Passes

	No. of Games	TD	Interceptions
Joe Montana, San Francisco	4	11	0
Terry Bradshaw, Pittsburgh	4	9	4
Roger Staubach, Dallas	4	8	4
Jim Plunkett, Oak-LA Raiders	2	4	0
Doug Williams, Washington	1	4	1

All-Time Super Bowl Leaders: Receiving

	No. of Games	No.	TD
Roger Craig, San Francisco	3	20	3
Jerry Rice, San Francisco	2	18	4
Lynn Swann, Pittsburgh	4	16	3
Chuck Foreman, Minnesota	3	15	0
Cliff Branch, Oak-LA Raiders	3	14	3

All-Time Super Bowl Leaders: Scoring

	Games	TD	FG	PAT	Pts.
Roger Craig, San Francisco	3	4	0	0	24
Franco Harris, Pittsburgh	4	4	0	0	24
Jerry Rice, San Francisco	2	4	0	0	24
Ray Wersching, San Francisco	2	0	5	7	22
Don Chandler, Green Bay	2	0	4	8	20

Glossary

BACKFIELD. The area behind the line of scrimmage where the quarterback and other backs set before the ball is snapped.

BLITZ. When one or more defensive backs charge the quarterback instead of covering downfield.

POCKET. The area formed by the offensive line around the quarterback once the ball is snapped.

SAFETY. A two-point play when the offense is downed in their own end zone.

SCRAMBLE. When the quarterback has to run around in the backfield to evade a tackle.

SCRIMMAGE LINE. The imaginary line where the football is placed between downs, separating the offensive and defensive teams.

Bibliography

Books

Meserole, Mike, ed. *The 1992 Information Please Sports Almanac.* Boston: Houghton Mifflin.

Sullivan, George. *All About Football.* New York: Dodd, Mead & Company: 1987.

The Official National Football League 1991 Record & Fact Book. New York: Workman Publishing Co.: 1991.

Periodicals

Albom, Mitch. "Super Bowl: 25th Anniversary Celebration." *Sports Illustrated*, January 14, 1991: 39.

Durbano, Art. "25 Most Memorable Moments From TV's Biggest Event." *TV Guide*, January 26, 1991: 4.

Jacobson, Steve. "What Makes It So Super?" *Sports Illustrated*, January 14, 1991: 64.

Miller, J. David. "XXV Things You Should Know About Super Bowl XXV." *Sport*, February 1991: 36.

"Super Bowl Madness." *Sport*, February 1990: 34.

Photo Credits

ALLSPORT USA: 6 (Rick Stewart); 26 (Otto Greule); 31 (T.G. Higgins); 33, 38 (J. Daniel); 35, 40 (Tim DeFrisco); 36, 42 (Mike Powell)
NFL Properties: 8 (Malcolm Emmons), 16 (Manny Rubio)
UPI/Bettmann Archive: 4, 13, 14, 19, 24, 29, 34
Wide World Photos: 12, 23

Index